W9-BPP-854

DISCARD

DISCARD

A Note to Parents

DK READERS is a compelling program for beginning readers, designed in conjunction with leading literacy experts, including Dr. Linda Gambrell, Professor of Education at Clemson University. Dr. Gambrell has served as President of the National Reading Conference and the College Reading Association, and the International Reading Association.

Beautiful illustrations and superb full-color photographs combine with engaging, easy-to-read stories to offer a fresh approach to each subject in the series. Each DK READER is guaranteed to capture a child's interest while developing his or her reading skills, general knowledge, and love of reading.

The five levels of DK READERS are aimed at different reading abilities, enabling you to choose the books that are exactly right for your child:

Pre-level 1: Learning to read
Level 1: Beginning to read
Level 2: Beginning to read alone
Level 3: Reading alone
Level 4: Proficient readers

The "normal" age at which a child begins to read can be anywhere from three to eight years old. Adult participation through the lower levels is very helpful for providing encouragement, discussing storylines, and sounding out unfamiliar words.

No matter which level you select, you can be sure that you are helping your child learn to read, then read to learn!

LONDON, NEW YORK, MUNICH,
MELBOURNE, AND DELHI

For Brady Games
Publisher David Waybright
Editor-in-Chief H. Leigh Davis
Publisher David Waybright
Licensing Director Mike Degler
Marketing Director Debby Neubauer
International Translations Brian Saliba
Title Manager Tim Fitzpatrick

For DK Publishing
Publishing Director Beth Sutinis
Reading Consultant
Linda Gambrell, Ph.D.

Produced by
Shoreline Publishing Group LLC
President James Buckley Jr.
Designer Tom Carling, carlingdesign.com

© 2008 DK/BradyGAMES, a division of Penguin Group (USA) Inc.
BradyGames® is a registered trademark of Penguin Group (USA)
Inc. All rights reserved, including the right of reproduction in whole
or in part in any form.

© 2008 Pokémon. © 1997–2008 Nintendo, Creatures, GAME
FREAK, TV Tokyo, Shopro, JR Kikaku. Pokémon properties are
trademarks of Nintendo

DK/BradyGAMES
800 East 96th St., 3rd floor
Indianapolis, IN 46240

08 09 10 11 10 9 8 7 6 5 4 3 2 1

A catalog record for this book is available from the Library of Congress.

ISBN: 978-0-7566-4431-4 (Paperback)
ISBN: 978-0-7566-4480-2 (Hardback)

Printed and bound by Lake Book.

Discover more at
www.dk.com

Contents

READING 3 ALONE

Become a
Pokémon Trainer

Written by Michael Teitelbaum

3 1389 01999 9929

DK
DK Publishing

What is a Pokémon Trainer?

Say hello to Professor Oak. He is a Pokémon expert. He's here to tell you about Pokémon Trainers.

Lots of Pokémon live in the wild. When they are caught, they need to be trained. That's the job of a Pokémon Trainer. What's a Pokémon Trainer?

A Pokémon Trainer is a person who dedicates his or her life to taking care of Pokémon. A Trainer collects Pokémon. He or she then teaches the Pokémon to use their abilities. One Trainer's Pokemon battle other Trainers' Pokemon. These battle can take place anywhere! But there is more to being a good Pokémon Trainer than battling. That's what this book is about.

Great Ball

Poké Ball

Luxury Ball

Net Ball

Repeat Ball

Master Ball

Pokémon Trainer Equipment

Before Pokémon Trainers can begin training their Pokémon, they need a few pieces of basic equipment. The first piece of equipment a Pokémon Trainer needs—and must learn to use—is a Poké Ball. Poké Balls are used to capture Pokémon in the wild.

Trainers throw their Poké Balls at wild Pokémon. If a Trainer is lucky, and the wild Pokémon is weak enough, it will be caught inside the Poké Ball. Only one Pokémon fits inside a Poké Ball. So Trainers should keep a good supply of Poké Balls on hand.

There are many different types of Poké Balls. Trainers choose the one that will work best for them each time.

As a Pokémon Trainer, once you first catch a wild Pokémon in a Poké Ball, that Pokémon might still escape. If it doesn't, then it is yours to train.

A well-trained Pokémon will leave its Poké Ball only when its Trainer tells it to. Pokémon usually can't get out of a Poké Ball by themselves.

Another important piece of equipment that every Pokémon Trainer needs is a Pokédex. A Pokédex contains lots

Inside a Poké Ball

of information about every single Pokémon. The more you know about your Pokémon, the better Trainer you will be.

Sinnoh Pokédex

Your Pokédex

When a Trainer begins his or her Pokémon journey, he or she receives a Pokédex. It is a portable encyclopedia all about Pokémon. When you find a Pokémon in the wild, pull out your Pokédex. In an instant you'll learn all about that Pokémon.

Trainers and their Pokémon

The relationships between Trainers and their Pokémon have many sides. Trainers catch Pokémon. They train them to battle. They take care of their Pokémon. And they become good friends with their Pokémon.

Piplup, Chimchar, and Turtwig

**Regions of
the Pokémon World**

The Pokémon world is
divided into regions. Each
region has lots of cities.
Some of the regions are
Kanto, Sinnoh, Johto,
Hoenn, Holon, and Orange Islands. Each region has
its own Pokémon and Pokémon contests.

The Sinnoh region

The journey to become a Pokémon Trainer begins when a person gets his or her first Pokémon. The new Pokémon Trainer usually chooses from a Fire-type, a Grass-type, or a Water-type Pokémon.

Trainers from the Kanto region come to Professor Oak to get their first Pokémon. They can choose from a Bulbasaur, a Charmander, or a Squirtle. Of course, different Trainers in different regions choose other Pokémon.

Now that you've chosen your first Pokémon, it's time to head out on your Pokémon journey. The next step is to catch Pokémon in the wild. When you spot a wild Pokémon, you send one or more of your Pokémon out to battle the wild Pokémon.

Once the wild Pokémon gets weak enough from the battle, it is ready to be caught. That's when you throw your Poké Ball. If the wild Pokémon is weak enough, it will be caught in your Poké Ball. Congratulations, you've caught you first wild Pokémon!

Now comes the most important part of being a Trainer: becoming friends with your new Pokémon. Your Pokémon will learn from you. You will also learn from your Pokémon.

Pokémon Types

Every Pokémon is identified by a type. The type tells you what kind of battle techniques the Pokémon uses. There are seventeen different Pokémon types. They are: Fire-type, Water-type,

Darkrai, a Dark-type

Grass-type, Electric-type, Normal-type, Ice-type, Fighting-type, Poison-type, Ground-type, Flying-type, Psychic-type, Bug-type, Rock-type, Ghost-type, Dragon-type, Dark-type, and Steel-type. Some Pokémon are more than one type. These are called "dual-type" Pokémon.

Gallade, a Psychic-and-Fighting-type

Lickilicky, a Normal-type

You will train your Pokémon to battle other Pokémon in gyms and in the wild. But you must never

force a Pokémon to do anything it isn't ready for.

You must consider the abilities of your Pokémon. Each Pokémon is unique and special. Treat it that way. If you use its particular talents, your Pokémon will grow stronger and happier.

Sure, it's fun to win battles and collect badges. But the friendship between Pokémon and their Trainers is far more important than the number of badges or battles they win.

A successful Trainer is not the one with the most Pokémon or the most badges. The best Trainers are the ones who treat their Pokémon with kindness and respect.

Gym Leaders

You've caught Pokémon. You've trained them. You've learned to care for them. Now it's time to test their skills in Pokémon gyms.

Most major cities in each region have a gym. Trainers bring their Pokémon to the gym to battle other Trainers' Pokémon.

Each gym has a Gym Leader. The Gym Leader is a very experienced Trainer. He or she has won many Pokémon battles. Young Trainers try their skill against Gym Leaders in order to improve. If you beat a Gym Leader, you earn a badge.

The badges show which Gym Leaders a Pokémon Trainer has defeated. Each type of badge is unique.

Brock, a Gym Leader, with his Pokémon

Every gym has a special badge. If a new Trainer beats a Gym Leader in that Leader's own gym, the Trainer wins a colorful badge. Each region in the Pokémon world has its own league. The league is made up of all the gyms in that region.

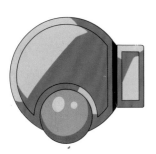

Hoenn League,
Knuckle Badge

Hoenn League,
Rain Badge

Orange League,
Sea Ruby Badge

Hoenn League,
Mind Badge

Johto League,
Raising Badge

One goal of a Pokémon Trainer is to beat each Gym Leader and win that gym's badge. Each badge shows that the Trainer has taken another step on his or her journey. When a Trainer wins every badge in a league, he or she is ready to move on to another region.

Hoenn League,
Heat Badge

Johto League,
Glacier Badge

Hoenn League,
Feather Badge

Orange League,
Coral-Eye Badge

Johto League,
Hive Badge

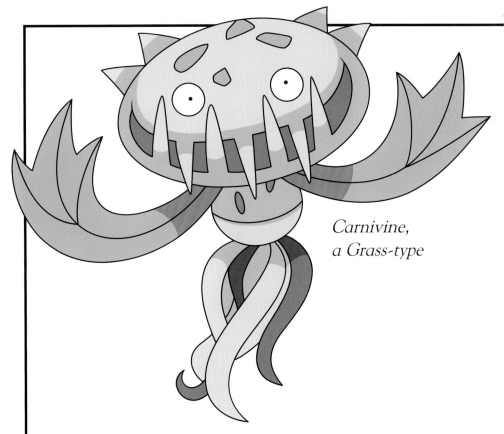

*Carnivine,
a Grass-type*

Most regions have eight Gym
Leaders—one for each gym. Once
a Trainer has beaten all eight Gym
Leaders in a region, earning all eight
badges, it's time to face the Elite
Four. The Elite Four are the four best
Pokémon Trainers in a region, aside
from the League Champion.

The members of the Elite Four train

all types of Pokémon. Just when you figure out how to beat one Trainer's Grass-types, you have to take on an Ice-type or Fire-type Pokémon next. That's why it's important for a Pokémon Trainer to collect Pokémon of all different types.

Then, it's important for the Trainer to choose the right Pokémon for each battle. Learning which of his or her Pokémon match up against the other Trainer's Pokémon is a big part of a Trainer's training.

Glaceon, an Ice-type

As you move up and win more battles, the job just gets tougher! For instance, in order to qualify to face the League Champion, you must battle and defeat all four members of the Elite Four. If you lose to any of them, you are eliminated from the tournament. It's a lot of hard work for you and all your Pokémon.

Steven Stone's Aggron

Wallace, a League Champion, and his Milotic

If you beat the Elite Four, you get to battle the Pokémon League Champion. If you win, you become the new League Champion, the highest level a Pokémon Trainer can reach in that region.

A Trainer who earns eight badges, defeats the Elite Four, and then becomes League Champion must defend the title!

Raichu

The Leagues

The goal of many Pokémon Trainers is to compete in a League Tournament.

The Kanto region's league is known as the Indigo League. Trainers who enter this tournament have to face eight tough Gym Leaders. Each one specializes in one type of Pokémon.

You'll find a variety of challenges. Take Lt. Surge in Vermilion City. He specializes in Electric-type Pokémon. He'll throw a supercharged Raichu at you. Then you'll have to face Erika, who trains Grass-type Pokémon in Celadon City. Watch out for her Gloom and its gross-smelling honey!

Gloom

If you make it past all eight Kanto Gym Leaders, you then face the Indigo League Elite Four. Loreli trains Ice-type Pokémon. Bruno trains Fighting-type Pokémon, such as Hitmonchan. Agatha trains Ghost-type Pokémon, such as Gengar. Finally, Lance trains Dragon-type Pokémon, such as Red Gyrados.

Gengar

If you compete in the Johto region, you start off facing Falkner in Violet City. Watch out for his Pidgeot; it can flap its wings and create powerful gusts of wind. If you beat him, you have seven more Gym Leaders to face in the Johto League. Becoming a League Champion isn't easy . . . but you can do it!

Hitmonchan

Brawly's Machop

Another region you might visit to challenge Gym Leaders is the Hoenn region. One of the top Gym Leaders in Hoenn's league is Brawly. He trains Fighting-type Pokémon. His Machop is a martial arts fighting machine! Pokémon Trainers who battle Brawly need to know how to take on Fighting-types.

You'll also have to face Flannery from Lavaridge. She is an expert on Fire-type Pokémon. Her red-hot Slugma is made out of super-hot lava!

What do you think will work well against Fire-type Pokémon? If you choose the right answer, you can win.

Then, if you get past all eight Hoenn League Gym Leaders, you face their Elite Four. Sidney is an expert on Dark-type Pokémon.

You could face his metal-bodied Metang. Its super-hard body can't be scratched or dented!

Sidney's Metang

Hoenn Elite Four member Phoebe is an expert on Ghost-type Pokémon. Battle her and you'll have to take on her Dusclops. If you don't pick the right Pokemon for the battle, Phoebe's powerful Dusclops will knock you out with Shadow Punch.

Phoebe's Dusclops

The Orange Crew

In the Orange Island League, you must battle and defeat four Orange Island Gym Leaders. They are known as the Orange Crew. There's Cissy in the Mikan Island Gym, Danny in the Navel Island Gym, Rudy in the Trovita Island Gym, and Luana in the Kumquat Island Gym.

Danny's Orange Island Gym

Next up is Glacia, who does her best when training Ice-type Pokemon such as her Spheal. Then comes Drake, who is an expert on Dragon-type Pokémon. Just try and crack his Shelgon's rugged shell.

In addition to the leagues in Kanto, Johto, and Hoenn, you can also compete in Pokémon leagues in the Sinnoh region and in the Orange Islands.

Whichever league you try, you'll face top Trainers!

Ash and Pikachu with the three Sinnoh Starters

Top Trainers

All Trainers start out at the same level. The better ones go on to win battles, get badges, and even win Pokémon tournaments.

Professor Oak's friend Ash Ketchum is from his hometown of Pallet Town. Ash is a great Trainer. No one is more dedicated to his Pokémon. He has traveled the world to increase his skills as a Pokémon Trainer. And he takes the time to help other Trainers.

For Ash, it's not about how many badges he wins, though he has won quite a few. It's all about his friendship with his Pokémon. Ash's first Pokémon was the Electric-type Pikachu, a funny but powerful Pokémon. Ash also has Squirtle and Charizard.

Ash's friend Misty is also a great Pokémon Trainer. Many Trainers work with several types of Pokémon. However, Misty chooses to focus on one type of Pokémon. She loves to train Water-type Pokémon. Misty and her sisters are the Gym Leaders at the Cerulean City gym. Misty's Pokémon include Staryu and Starmie, which are, of course, Water-type Pokémon.

Ash and Misty's friend Brock is not only a great Trainer, but he was a Gym Leader. He is well on his way to becoming a master Pokemon Breeder. He knows

Staryu

all about breeding, training, and caring for Pokémon. He's also the Gym Leader at the Pewter City gym.

While Misty loves Water-types, Brock loves Rock-type Pokémon. Two of the Pokémon he works with often are Geodude and Onix.

Starmie

Professor Oak's grandson, Gary Oak, is a very good Pokémon Trainer. But he didn't start out that way. At first, he was something of a bully. He could be rude. He cared more about how many badges he won and how many Pokémon he caught. Acting like that is not how the best Pokémon Trainers do their jobs.

But his skills were never in doubt. In time, Gary realized that caring for

Pokémon Professors

Pokémon professors know a lot about the Pokémon in their region. But, of course, they are always enthusiastic to learn more. They also give out starter Pokémon to new Trainers. They include Professor Ivy of the Orange Islands, Professor Elm of the Johto region, and Professor Rowan of the Sinnoh region *(left)*.

Gary Oak started as a Trainer, but now has a new job.

Pokémon is the most important thing for a Trainer.

Recently, he retired from Pokémon competitions. He's become a Pokémon researcher, just like Professor Oak! Gary works with Pokémon of many types. He tries to learn even more of their amazing secrets!

When a young girl named May started out as a Trainer, she was a little bit afraid of her Pokémon. As she spent more time training her first Pokémon, Torchic, she realized that she wasn't interested in using her Pokémon in battles. Instead, she entered Pokemon Contests as a Contest Coordinator. Coordinators use Pokemon and their abilities in amazing ways.

May and Torchic

The goal of a Contest is to show off the beauty and strength of Pokemon by combining moves in artistic and unique ways. Trainers and their Pokémon work hard to win ribbons in these contests.

A Pokémon Contest does not focus on battles. The Pokémon and their Trainers match up in other ways, including energy and talent. Contests are another great way to have fun!

Pokémon Contests

Some Trainers prefer to enter their Pokémon in Pokémon Contests rather than Pokémon battles. In a Pokémon Contest, Trainers get to show off what good shape their Pokémon are in. They also show off their best moves. In a Pokémon Contest, style counts more than victory in a battle.

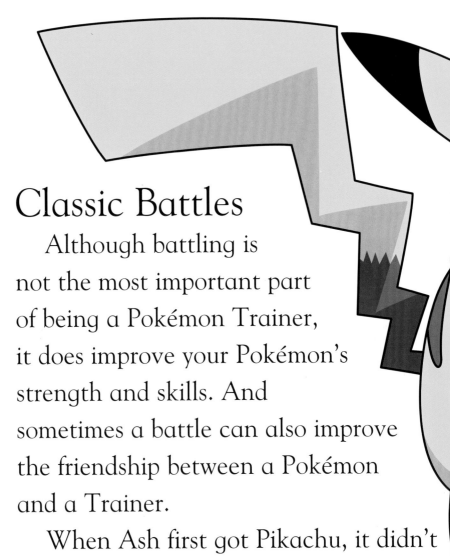

Classic Battles

Although battling is
not the most important part
of being a Pokémon Trainer,
it does improve your Pokémon's
strength and skills. And
sometimes a battle can also improve
the friendship between a Pokémon
and a Trainer.

When Ash first got Pikachu, it didn't
obey him at all. Then, the two new
partners were attacked by a flock of wild
Spearow. Ash put himself in danger to

save Pikachu.

Pikachu realized how much Ash really cared. Then Pikachu used its Thunder Shock attack to defeat the Spearow. A beautiful friendship between Pokémon and Trainer was born.

Articuno

One time, Ash battled a Trainer
named Noland in the Battle Frontier.
Noland worked with a Legendary
Pokémon called Articuno. Ash used
his Charizard. Charizard attacked with

Legendary Pokémon

The Legendary Pokémon are a group
of rare and powerful Pokémon. They
will appear only to special Trainers.
Very few people have ever seen
them. Articuno, Zapdos, Moltres,
Mew, and Mewtwo (*left*) are some of
the most famous.

Flamethrower. Articuno countered with an Ice Beam. Charizard took the match with an earth-shaking Seismic Toss.

Another classic battle took place when two Legendary Pokémon faced off. Long ago, the Legendary Pokémon Groudon and Kyogre had a battle that almost destroyed the world. They recently fought again using Hyper Beam and Solar Beam attacks. The battle ended in a tie again!

Charizard

Once, Professor Oak's grandson Gary faced Ash in a huge six-on-six battle at the Silver Conference. Gary used Nidoqueen, Magmar, Scizor, Golem, Arcanine, and Blastoise. Ash countered with Tauros, Heracross, Muk, Bayleef, Snorlax, and Charizard. In the end, Ash finally beat his biggest rival.

Snorlax

Sometimes Pokémon Trainers battle their friends. When Ash fought his good friend Misty, Ash used his Kingler. But just when it looked like he would win, Misty's Psyduck accidentally came out of its Poké Ball to take the battle for Misty.

Scizor

So, now that you have learned all about what it takes to be a Pokémon Trainer, do you want to become one? Of course you do! The road is long, and there is much hard work to do. But in the end, it's worth it.

You'll start out with one Pokémon and add more and more as you move through the Pokémon world.

If you work hard and do your best—and take care of your Pokémon—you might move up.

You might be good enough to become a Gym Leader, or a member of the Elite Four, or even a Pokémon League Champion. You might become a Pokémon Coordinator and compete in contests. Or you might become a Pokémon professor like Professor Oak!

Dawn, Ash and Pikachu

But whatever you choose, the journey will be worthwhile as you and your Pokémon become the best of friends.

Glossary

Abilities
Things that a person—or a Pokémon—can do very well or can do better than most.

Badges
Special awards given to Pokémon Trainers for defeating certain Gym Leaders.

Challenger
Someone who hopes to defeat a champion to take that person's place as the new champion.

Congratulations
Good wishes given to someone who has won something or who has achieved a at feat.

Dedicate
To choose to follow something through to the end.

Eliminate
To remove, to get rid of.

Encyclopedia
A book or electronic device containing detailed information on a subject or subjects.

Identify
To give something a label, to figure out what something is.

Gusts
Strong blasts of air, usually caused by wind.

Lava
Boiling hot liquid rock.

Martial arts
A skilled system of fighting.

Qualify
Earn a place in something by your achievements.

Researcher
Someone who studies a subject to learn new information about that subject.

Rival
An opponent, a competitor.

Seismic
Having to do with the movement of the interior parts of the earth.

Supercharged
Filled with power or energy.

Techniques
Skills or methods of doing something.

Void
A place of emptiness.

Worthwhile
Important, worth doing.

Index